Super Cool Science

SOUTH POLE STATION

PAST, PRESENT, AND FUTURE

Sandra Markle

WALKER AND COMPANY
NEW YORK

For Guy Guthridge, in appreciation for all his help.

The author would like to thank the National Science Foundation for sponsoring her visit to the South Pole. Thanks also go to the following individuals for their many contributions to this project: Frank Brier, David Bubenheim, Eric Cheng, Dave Grisez, Al Harper, Kate Jensen, Jerry Marty, William McAfee, Robert Morse, John Rand, Kathie Sharp, Neil Sullivan, Al Sutherland.

Photo credits:
David Bubenheim: 25; Feraro-Choi and Association, Ltd., for National Science Foundation: 26, 27; Dave Grisez: 6; Sandra Markle: 3, 4, 5, 15, 23, 29; William McAfee: front cover, 11, 18, 19, 24, 30, 31, back cover; Robert Morse: title page, 20; National Science Foundation: 10, 28; and John Rand, National Science Foundation: 7, 8, 9, 12, 13, 14, 16, 17, 22.

First published in the United States of America in 1998 by Walker Publishing Company, Inc.

Published simultaneously in Canada by Thomas Allen & Son Canada, Limited, Markham, Ontario

Library of Congress Cataloging-in-Publication Data
Markle, Sandra.
Super cool science: South Pole stations, past, present, and future/Sandra Markle.
p. cm.
Includes bibliographical references and index.
Summary: Text and photographs tell the story of science research stations at the South Pole, including the one currently under construction, which will launch a new era of science.
ISBN 0-8027-8470-4 (hardcover). —ISBN 0-8027-8471-2 (reinforced)
1. Laboratories—South Pole—Juvenile literature. 2. Research—South Pole—Juvenile literature.
[1. Research—South Pole. 2. South Pole.] I. Title.
Q180.56.M37 1997
507.2098'9—dc21   97—14890
                                                                CIP
                                                                AC

Book design by Mspace

Printed in Hong Kong
10 9 8 7 6 5 4 3 2 1

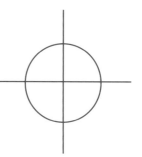

WELCOME TO THE SOUTH POLE

Hello. I'm Sandra Markle, and that's me at the South Pole, one of the coldest, windiest, wildest places on Earth. Check out what I am standing on—ice. At the South Pole, the ground is covered by a sheet of ice so thick it would take about 500 school buses stacked end to end to reach from the Earth's surface to the top. The ice never melts away because it is freezing cold year-round. This picture was taken on a sunny, summer South Pole day when the temperature warmed up to −25°F (-32°C).

So why did I travel to the cold, frozen South Pole? Something very exciting is happening there. Turn the page, and I'll tell you about it.

People first went to the South Pole because it was an unexplored frontier. Then scientists discovered the South Pole environment's unique qualities, including: unusually clean, dry air; night that lasts for months on end; a huge, clear ice sheet; and the harshest environment on the planet. This discovery launched a whole new kind of exploration at the South Pole—scientific investigations—and to conduct them, scientists needed a station. This is what the station currently looks like at the South Pole, but soon the United States' National Science Foundation (NSF) will build a brand-new station.

The new station will be the most high-tech research station ever built at the South Pole. It will actually be the third station. The first was started in 1956 when there was nothing there at all but ice as far as you could see in any direction. There was no marker showing the location of the South Pole. To pinpoint this location—where the station was to be built—the construction crew used the same sort of navigational tools that sailors use to find their position far out at sea.

THE FIRST SOUTH POLE STATION

This is a picture of the first station, taken from an airplane on December 4, 1956, during the Antarctic summer construction season (the seasons there are the opposite of ours in the Northern Hemisphere). The dark triangles are tents where the construction crew slept. See the hut with the curved roof? That kind of building is called a *Jamesway*, and it was the main part of the first official station. The station was completed in time to begin exploration of the South Pole during the International Geophysical Year (IGY) 1957. This was a year scientists around the world set aside for investigating the Earth in new ways. The station was named the Amundsen-Scott Station after Roald Amundsen, who led the first expedition to reach the South Pole on December 14, 1911, and Robert Scott, whose expedition arrived 34 days later on January 17, 1912.

Take a closer look at the Jamesway, and you will discover it is only canvas stretched over supporting ribs. Both ends and the floor are wood. Several more Jamesways were built in order to expand the station. Even though the ice sheet on which they were building was uneven, the new Jamesways were constructed so their roofs were at exactly the same height as the main building. Paul Siple, who was overseeing construction, believed this would let the blowing snow sweep across the roofs rather than pile up on top of any one building.

If you live where it snows in the winter, your house roof probably has a steep pitch to let snow slide off. A heavy snow load can crush a roof.

now, peek inside a Jamesway at the first station. Imagine spending a nine-month-long winter here when the temperature outdoors is colder than your refrigerator's freezer! The wind would often be howling, and it would be dark for months on end.

To find out why it is dark all the time during the Antarctic winter, try this: Have someone hold a basketball or a soccer ball while you shine a flashlight at the middle of the ball from a few feet away. Now, have your partner tip the ball until the top is in shadow. The Earth is tipped as it orbits the sun. So when it is winter in Antarctica, the South Pole is dark. When it is summer in Antarctica, the South Pole is tipped toward the sun, and it is light all the time.

Compare these two views inside one of the first station's tunnels, and you will discover a serious problem that developed. How has the tunnel changed?

It rarely snows at the South Pole, but the wind blows hard nearly all the time. This wind sweeps the snow and ice along until it runs into something like one of the station's buildings. Then the wind slows and dumps its snow load. Despite lots of digging out, it was impossible to stop the first South Pole Station from slowly being buried and crushed. By 1966, plans were being made to replace the first South Pole Station.

1957

1990

THE SECOND SOUTH POLE STATION

Check out the artist's drawing of the second station, the one currently in operation. The main part of the station with living quarters, dining hall, offices, and a small recreation area is covered by a big metal *dome*. Though unheated, just by blocking out the wind and trapping some of the heat radiating from the buildings, the dome's interior is as much as 20 degrees warmer than the outside temperature—an important difference during the winter when temperatures can plummet to -100°F (-73° C). The dome and arch system also lets the station crew access the power plant, reach stored food, and repair broken equipment even when windblown snow makes it impossible to see, let alone work, outdoors.

The first station was primarily a military base where eighteen hardy explorers could live while probing this remarkable frontier. The second South Pole Station, though, is a research facility where thirty researchers and crew can live while investigating the Pole's unique environment.

To build the second station, plane load after plane load of equipment and building supplies had to be transported to the South Pole. New Jamesways were set up to house the large number of construction workers needed to build the station. Finally, during the 1970–71 Antarctic summer season, work began, and building continued for the next four summers. If that seems like a long time, remember, the construction season at the South Pole is only three months long.

The dome was finished first. It is 165 feet (50 meters) in diameter at the base and 55 feet (17 meters) high at the center. The metal tower you can see in the middle of this construction photo was removed once the framework was complete. Then, except for an opening at the very top, the dome was covered with aluminum panels.

Next, the arches were finished. This picture of one of the arches being built was taken from the top of the dome. First, equipment was set in place. Then the covering arch was built. Unlike the dome, the arches are made out of steel. See the big crane that was used to hoist the heavy equipment? In the background, you can see piles of lumber and other building supplies.

Compare these two views of the second South Pole Station. One shows how it looked in January 1975 when it was newly completed, and the other shows how it looked when I visited in January 1996. How has it changed?

1975

1996

Like the first station, the second South Pole Station is being buried. Despite digging out and plowing snow away each summer, drifting snow has built up more than 15 feet (5 meters) deep around the outside of the dome. So scientists are once again planning a new South Pole Station, the third one. Another reason for building a new station is to meet the demand for more beds, laboratories with high-tech equipment, more electricity, a better communication system—all the things needed to expand the opportunities for scientific research.

By the way, if you are wondering what ever happened to the first station, take a look. That station is now buried except for the tops of chimney pipes and antennas. In time, it will be completely buried.

$\mathcal{S}$UPPORTING NEW RE$\mathcal{S}$EARCH

One of the earliest research projects at the South Pole started because scientists are concerned about the Earth's *atmosphere,* the gases that form a life-supporting envelope around our planet. How polluted is our atmosphere? Is it more polluted in some places than others? Is the amount of carbon dioxide in the atmosphere increasing? To answer these questions and more, scientists from the National Oceanic and Atmospheric Administration (NOAA) started studying the Pole's superclean air so they could compare it to air from more populated places.

The South Pole Station itself, though, gives off some gases, heat, and humidity. That is what formed the cloud in this picture. So NOAA built the station's first separate research facility some distance away upwind.

These researchers are launching a balloon to carry instruments into the upper atmosphere to study the Earth's *ozone* layer. Ozone is a molecule made up of three oxygen atoms. High in the atmosphere, ozone absorbs most of the sun's ultraviolet (UV) radiation before it reaches Earth. Exposure to UV rays can damage plants and cause some people to develop skin cancer. Under normal conditions, there are as many new ozone molecules forming as there are old ones breaking down. But chemicals from aerosol cans, factories, and automobile exhausts rise into the atmosphere and break down ozone. Because air currents just naturally flow toward the North and South Poles, this problem is worse over the Poles. Sometimes there is so little ozone in the upper atmosphere, scientists say there is an ozone hole.

Scientists predict that within a few years the ozone problem should begin to improve due to pollution control efforts. To support expanded research, construction of the new high-tech Clean Air Facility is already under way. It will be one of the first parts of the new South Pole Station to be in operation.

As cities grew bigger, city lights, pollution, and water vapor made it harder for even the best telescopes in populated parts of the world to get a clear view of the stars. So astronomers traveled to Antarctica to set up their equipment. Because the air is clean and dry in Antarctica and night lasts for months at a time, astronomers are able to watch stars twenty-four hours a day!

The South Pole Station gives off some light and humidity, though. So the telescopes are located in the "Dark Sector," an area just far enough away from the main station to be unaffected by lights and radiated heat and humidity.

What looks like a cap and wooden cone are shields around two of the telescopes, protecting them from wind-blown ice crystals. The South Pole telescopes are nicknamed COBRA, SPIREX, and AST/RO. They let astronomers study the stars, but not by looking at them the way you do with your eyes. Besides visible light, most stars give off other forms of energy, such as X rays, ultraviolet rays, infrared rays, and radio waves. The energy signals are picked up by the South Pole telescopes and fed into computers, which produce images people can see and study.

Shortly after SPIREX became operational in 1995, it became the only telescope on Earth able to detect and record images of a comet smashing into the planet Jupiter.

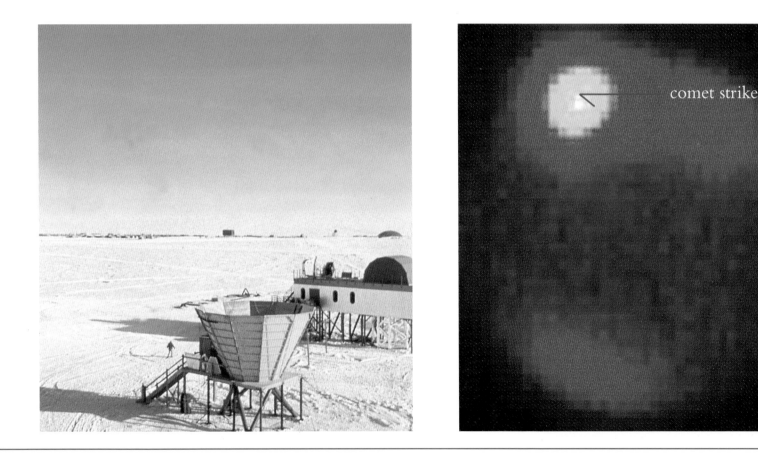

comet strike

This shiny ball is one of hundreds of strings of electricity sensors that were lowered into mile-deep holes drilled into the South Pole's ice sheet. When water that was pumped into these holes froze, the strings of sensors were anchored, creating a super tool, nicknamed AMANDA. AMANDA helps astronomers locate exploding stars in space.

To see how this cool tool works, draw six vertical straight lines in a row on a sheet of paper. Next, draw a diagonal line across the six lines. Particles from an exploding star normally pass through the Earth unnoticed, but those that bump into atoms give off tiny amounts of electricity. Each of AMANDA's sensors, which detect electricity, sends a signal to a computer. Like the line you drew, this computer traces the path of the particles across AMANDA's array of sensors, through the Earth, and out into space. Then astronomers use this path to aim their telescopes at the source of the particles—the exploding star.

The colorful lights in this picture are called *auroras*. An aurora forms when *solar wind,* the electrically charged particles from the sun, bumps into gases in the Earth's atmosphere. High in the atmosphere, oxygen atoms give off a red light. Lower down, oxygen atoms emit green light, and nitrogen emits blue light. The long, dark Antarctic winter is perfect for studying the beautiful auroras.

Some scientists study auroras just because they are fascinating. Others want to find a way to prevent auroras from interfering with radio and satellite communication. Still others wonder if this energy could be harnessed.

The South Pole's extreme environment makes it the perfect place to test systems being designed to support space exploration. This is a Controlled Ecological Life Support System (CELSS), a controlled climate chamber, that works like the much bigger one to be built at the new station. The CELSS will produce potatoes, lettuce, peppers, zucchini, strawberries—any fruits or vegetables that will do well in the limited space. In the process, the CELSS will also help recycle the station's sewage, using the liquid sewage stream in the growth chamber. Water vapor given off by the plants can be collected and cooled, producing fresh liquid water that is pure enough to drink. Meanwhile, solid sewage will be burned, producing an ash that can be used for fertilizer in the CELSS. What works at the South Pole may one day also help support explorers on Mars.

INSIDE THE NEW STATION

This is an artist's drawing of what the new South Pole Station will look like. You can probably guess why each building is called a "C." The station will start with just two buildings, called Pod A and Pod B.

Like the current station, all the exterior doors on the new station will be heavy metal freezer locker doors. Take a close look, though, and you will see something the new station will have that the current station lacks—windows.

Something else the new station will have that the current station lacks is fully equipped, high-tech science laboratories as well as private work stations for scientists. There also will be a teleconferencing center. And there will be many more bedrooms—enough for 150 people to have comfortable private rooms during the summer research season. There are 145 people who now squeeze into the current station. This number includes groups bunking in a summer-only dorm and the old Jamesways, which do not even have bathrooms. The winter-over crew will expand from a current maximum of 30 to 50 people in the new station.

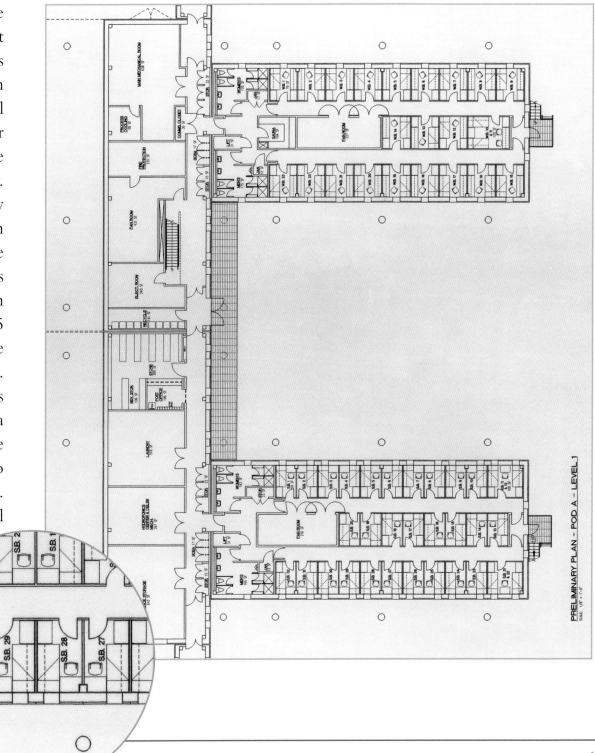

PRELIMINARY PLAN - POD A - LEVEL 1
SCALE 1/8" = 1'-0"

What looks like a big water bed is one of the fuel storage bladders in the cargo arches. The arches will continue to be used for maintenance and to store cargo and fuel for the power plant. Although solar panels will help supply heat and electricity during the summer, the primary power source for the new South Pole Station will still be diesel electric generators. The fuel to run the generators is JP-8, a mixture of antifreeze and jet fuel that is hauled to the station a little at a time by the planes arriving during the summer. Then it is stored in the giant fuel bladders.

The new station will be away from the arches, keeping it safe in case of fire. But the station will be connected to the arches by tunnels carved through the ice by this strange-looking machine.

When the new station is complete, the dome will be removed because it encourages drifting—something the new buildings are designed to resist. Roof edges facing into the wind will slope to deflect the wind under the buildings. This will let the wind blow on through rather than slow down and dump snow. But even with its drift-resistant shape, ice and snow are expected to pile up at a rate of 10 to 12 inches (25 to 30 centimeters) a year. So the new station buildings will be on legs. The legs are designed to lengthen, so when the ice gets too close, they will be able to lift the buildings up higher.

It is expected to take eight years to finish the new South Pole Station, but when completed it will have the capacity to launch a new era of science. For the first time, scientists from other countries may be invited to do research, making South Pole science truly a global effort.

Scientific research is also likely to expand in new directions. For example, scientists are wondering: What is the land like under the ice? Could there be tiny microbes living at the South Pole? To what extent are pollutants from the rest of the world reaching the Pole? If you could go to the South Pole, what would you like to investigate? Think about it. One day you could be doing super cool science at the new South Pole Station.

GLOSSARY / INDEX